Finding Yours Truly; a Journey of Self Discovery

Charissa Stuart

Presentation by *BookLeaf Publishing*

Web: www.bookleafpub.com

E-mail: info@bookleafpub.com

ISBN: 978-93-95784-12-2

First edition 2022

DEDICATION

For my husband,

who lifts me up when I am down

And

For my children,

who bring meaning to my world

ACKNOWLEDGEMENT

To my husband, who held my hand as I took a leap, and gave me the courage to fly, this book would not exist without you.

To the writing challenge that lit the fire within, thank you. You gave me the push I needed to do something more.

And to the reader, without you, these are just words in my head and written across my heart. You give these words a voice and make them real.

PREFACE

Where do you go, and what do you do when all your dreams have come to fruition?

I realised my life plan earlier than expected; got the man, the kids, the house, the dog. Tick, tick, tick. When I ran out of life goals I was left with a dilemma; What are you supposed to do with your life when you've done everything you set out to do? What comes next? Was this it? The culmination of my life's experiences? What is left to do but endure? I needed to shake things up. To begin a new adventure, to try something new.

If you're reading this, you are probably searching for your own 'what's next'. You are longing for something more. You are searching for self.

One day, while scrolling endlessly on social media, I came across a writing challenge. Three weeks, a poem a day, no holds barred, just write. I was intrigued. I began searching my existence for what comes after, and lines of poetry began filling my head. Thus; Finding Yours Truly was born.

Finding Yours Truly; a Journey of Self Discovery was my own personal quest to express my desire for something more. This challenge woke me up. It lit a fire within that had almost been extinguished by the drudgery of everyday life. Through taking this journey of exploration, I found there was more inside than I had realised, and it gave me the freedom to try to change.

Through looking within, I found inspiration. Now I hope my inspiration can be the catalyst for change for your own journey of self discovery, and bring you the comfort I discovered.

Are you ready?

The Challenge

What is this feeling
  Of untapped potential
    Of yearning for something more?

Finding My Voice

They say to start writing
To put pen to paper
And just write the things on your mind
But what if those things you are yearning to say
Are suddenly too hard to find?
You say what you say
And write what you write
And hope that it all turns out fine
Then you read what you wrote
And hear what's been said
And feel like you've run out of time
To truly write something of meaning
And hopefully someday inspire
That what has been said
Helps to clear out your head
And starts to fulfil your desire
To find the voice that's been missing
And figure out something to say
Continue the journey you've started to take
And see at the end of the day
That what you were fearing
Was not worth the fear
There's comfort in finding your way
So do the thing you're avoiding
Just start

And soon you will see
That there's more to be had by beginning a task
Than there is by letting things be

Living The Life Fulfilled

There is more to life than unfilled potential
There is more than the doom and the gloom
There is comfort here in a life worth living
There is sunshine
        And flowers
           And warmth
              And forgiving
With children half grown
        Coming into their own
There is comfort in building our home

Breaking Free

Brace yourself for the forward momentum
Take a leap into the unknown
Take just one step
        Then another step more
'Til you've spread your wings and you've flown
    Beyond the barriers
       You've had in the past
    And into the freedom
       That's now within grasp
As you take one step after another
    On the pathway of personal growth

Peaceful Surrender

Live in the moment
One step at a time
No thoughts of tomorrow
Of losing your mind
Live in the present
   Be open
    Begin
Feel the peaceful surrender
That comes from within

Acceptance

Acceptance
That feeling of letting things be
Acceptance
Of looking to see what you see
Acceptance
Of being okay with just me
Acceptance

Satisfied

That feeling of completeness
That feeling of whole
That comes with acceptance
And fleeting control
That feeling of peaceful
Of filling the hole
That feeling of comfort
In healing your soul
That feeling that comes
At the end of the day
To wipe all your worries
And sorrows away
Satisfaction

Say Something

Say something more than you've said in the past
Say something slightly unsure
Say something brave you're afraid to display
Something you feel to your core

Say something slightly sensational
Say something real that's impressive
Something enchanting that's truly outstanding
Say something kind of excessive

Say something silently savage
Then vocally say something kind
Say something building up others
Say the best thing that springs to your mind

Say something so systematically
Thought out and ordered just so
Say something planned that is high in demand
Something that helps you to grow

Say something freeing
Say something new
Say something deep down within
Say something vast from inside of your heart

Say something as you begin
To say something inspirational
Say something more than before
Say something bigger
Say something well
Take a deep breath
And have something to tell
Say something
        Say something
                Say something

Torn

Accepting the challenge to change
Needs a little more day after day
But figuring out what to change
Is the challenge that gets in the way
Where you know that something needs changing
But deciding on what that should be
Is the biggest part of the journey
In trying to figure out me

Two Sides

There are two sides to every coin
Opposites? You know there are two
  Two wheels on a bike
    Two wings on a bird
And two choices when seeing things through

For without two sides of a coin
There's not really chance anymore
For a coin with one face
    Rigs the game
      Wins the race
And makes every outcome for sure

The opposite of absent is present
  The opposite of daytime is night
The opposite of sadness is joy, and
  The opposite of darkness is light

A flying bird needs both wings to fly
A bike needs two wheels to be free
And although a unicycle exists
  It is better to let that one be

When faced with the option of moving ahead
You can go or let fear make you stay

But if you decide to move out of fears grasp
You're suddenly one step away

From taking the ride of your life; feel alive
And spreading your wings; take a leap
And fly out into the crazy unknown
         Wake up from being asleep

There are two sides to every coin
Take a chance and soon you will see
It is better to live the adventure
Feel the freedom it is to be free

Hope

The first glimmer of light at dawn
The peeping of seedlings through snow
The sighting of land after being at sea
That feeling that comes as you grow

Finding that you are no longer withdrawn
Your confidence builds from within
The change that occurs
                    as you start to mature
And your life is about to begin

There is hope growing slowly but surely
For a future that's only a dream
But given the chance
                With some time
                        And hard work
That future can come into being

Hope helps you build something better
Hope stays with you in the endeavour
Hope helps you to act on the dreaming
Hope gives to the present some meaning

So find your hope for tomorrow
    Take a chance

Give it time
Do the work
Trust in the future you're seeking
And build something truely of worth

Opening Up

The possibilities that come from opening up
Being open to new adventure
And open to something more
Fills the void inside you never knew existed

The deep chasm
While scary in its initial vastness
Suddenly becomes a world of opportunity
A place for exploration
A place for growth
For soul searching
And discovery
Finding things you didn't know were missing

When you realise the hole does in fact exist
And become open for ways to fill the crack
You find new meaning
And hope
And enlightenment

When the rift inside is beginning to heal
You find that it wasn't a wound at all
But a place for personal journey
And inner peace

Inner Strength

Doing the thing that needs to be done
When you don't have the strength to carry on
Takes courage that's found
Through a battle hard-won
Inner strength

Choosing to search for your own inner light
Allowing your heart to slowly take flight
Not knowing if it will turn out alright
Inner strength

Even when you've been through an ordeal
Allowing the time that it takes you to heal
Not knowing if healing is actually real
Inner strength

Defining Moments

You know those moments in life
When everything around you is crumbling
And in the midst of trouble and heartache
You somehow find the strength to carry on?

In managing to face the impossible
Your true nature is revealed
And in the revealing you discover
The measure of who you truly are

Yet without those catastrophic moments
The ones that make you grow
Your inner self would be left
Lacking development

So as much as you wish for an easy journey
As much as you long for peace
You need life's defining moments
To teach
        And develop
                Your true self

Flying

Longing for adventure
You take a leap
And instead of falling
Something miraculous occurs
Suddenly you feel yourself lifted up
As if carried on a cloud
And before you know it you're flying
High above the ground
Living your new adventure
While initially daunting
You revel in your newfound freedom

Flying high above it all
You consider what you've left behind
And see your life unfolding
As if floating on a dream
Learning from the lessons past
You use the grand experience
To build your self esteem
As you rise higher and higher
You realise this is what you've been missing
This is what you've been searching for
Living for tomorrow
You're free

Chasing Happiness

Run, don't walk, just run
Beyond the limits implied
Move towards the horizon
Feel the power that's building inside

Chase the future that you can imagine
Live out the life you deserve
It is more than okay to strive for your dreams
Don't settle for what you've been served

See the happiness just up ahead
Reach for it, don't let it go
Take a leap into the unknown
Experience change as you grow

Never Give Up

Never give up on your journey to change
Do what it takes to improve
Never be scared of the journey ahead
Do all that you can to remove
All of the fears that are holding you back
And all of the doubt left inside
Never give up on your feelings of hope
Do what it takes to survive
Never, no never give up

Closure

At the end of the day
When all's said and done
There is great satisfaction
In a journey well won
Through all of the struggles
And longing to change
If you've put in the work
And let fear drift away
There is something enchanting
In a dream life fulfilled
And something accomplished
Through climbing uphill
And facing the hardships
Life's thrown in your way
There is joy in the journey
You took yesterday

When looking back
On the things you have done
You realise that
You have only begun
To live your own great adventure
And discover all that entails
Live in the moment
And truly be free

And feel what it means
To be fine with just me

When you find your true self
On the journey you've made
You recognise that
You're no longer afraid
To be all you've ever
Wanted to be
And find closure
In walking
The pathway
To me

The Journey To Here

It's easy enough to look back in time
And understand things retrospectively
It's harder to learn from the here and the now
When you're searching for your lost identity

Seeing the past through the hindsight of now
Helps you to answer the question of how
How did that happen
          And what did you learn
How did you get here
          And where you should turn

When you examine the journey you're on
You realise that you have only begun
To put things into perspective
          And hopefully feel more alive
To learn from the lessons
          You've had from the past
And do what you need to survive

So how to move on
Without knowing what's next
How do you face the unknown
By looking back at the things that you've done
And seeing how strong you have grown

Moving Ahead

When you've achieved
All you've tried to achieve
With all your desires fulfilled
The questions arise as to moving ahead
And what further dreams to pursue

How to move forward
When reaching your goals
Start by enjoying the present
Revel in all your accomplishments past
Then find something new to develop

Begin by choosing a whole new adventure
Build on the dreams of before
Move beyond with this forward momentum
And grow just a little bit more

Finding Yours Truly

Finding myself on the pathway to me
Was an outcome quite unexpected
It led me to wonder and act more alive
It helped me to feel more connected

This journey of self discovery
Woke me up from being asleep
And as I found more and more freedom
It left me feeling complete

Finding yours truly while searching within
Put an end to my trying to hide
It gave me the power to take back my life
Filled the part that was missing inside

www.ingramcontent.com/pod-product-compliance
Lightning Source LLC
Chambersburg PA
CBHW060924130726
48001CB00006B/2415